household management for men

First published in Great Britain in 2004 by
Cassell Illustrated, a division of
Octopus Publishing Group Ltd
2-4 Heron Quays
London
E14 4JP

A CIP catalogue record for this book is
available from the British Library.

ISBN 1-84403273-6
9781844032730

Conceived, designed and produced by
Quid Publishing
Fourth Floor
Sheridan House
112-116A Western Road
Hove BN3 1DD
England
www.quidpublishing.com

Publisher: Nigel Browning
Publishing Manager: Sophie Martin
Author: Jane Moseley
Project Management: Essential Works
Illustrations: Matt Pagett

Printed and bound in China by
Midas Printing International Ltd

NOTE
Every effort has been taken to ensure that
all information in this book is correct and
compatible with national standards at the
time of publication. This book is not
intended to replace manufacturers'
instructions in the use of their tools or
products – always follow their safety
guidelines.

bedroom

household management for men

Contents

Bedroom

'A captain in the kitchen is often
a brigadier in the bedroom.'
A ELLIS

The Art and Science of Domestic Wisdom

Let's start with a few little-known but interesting facts. Household management is both a science and an art; it uses both sides of the male brain and is a practical and spiritual exercise – practical because it establishes order, hygiene and safety within the home environment; spiritual because it makes you feel more comfortable and secure within your own four walls (plus rather pleased with yourself). Even better, housework is also an aerobic exercise that allows you to flex your muscles and push your weight about at home without annoying people.

Housework is not dull, boring or a waste of leisure hours that could be better spent in front of a television or at the bar. It saves time, creates order out of chaos, burns calories and makes you sexier. Are you more interested now? Read on.

Men, when questioned about how much housework they do, often reply: 'Not my department,' 'Far too busy at work,' 'What's the point? It always looks the same five minutes later,' and 'Do you reckon Hercules did the dusting?' However, in our fast-changing world, increasing numbers of men share the household chores or, indeed, assume full responsibility for them. The dynamics are changing. Real men do housework – it's a fact. And real men get rewards.

The Little Book of Domestic Wisdom demonstrates how to approach household tasks positively and effectively, how to schedule, organize and execute tasks efficiently – just like any other job that lands in the daily in-tray – and shows how to enjoy a similar sense of achievement and fulfillment. Some jobs are more rewarding than others: dusting, like filing, can pile up and stare you in the face for some time without any major repercussions, but neglecting the kitchen sink or the laundry basket will lead to instant inconvenience. However, just think how great you feel when the filing tray is empty. It's the same with housework. And you haven't got the journey home afterwards.

What to do when

Don't let the very thought of housework overwhelm you, just like a huge work project upon which you cannot get started. Ease yourself into it and do a little each day. Don't wait until things get completely out of control before tackling them – tasks will take twice the amount of time and be half as effective. To do it properly you need a system, a routine and a schedule. 'Diarize, prioritize, realize' is a good mission statement – it works just as well at home as on the time management course and in the office.

First things first

Individuals should assume responsibility for their own clutter. Taking ownership of a problem is half way to solving it. Admitting to ownership of a pair of odorous socks under the sofa is the first step on the road to removing, washing and putting back in the bedroom. Don't upset people by de-junking their possessions without consultation. It would be like reading their post and dumping it without their knowledge or consent. Set a time schedule for the 'house de-junk' and stick to it.

If some tasks are going to take more than a few days (eg clearing an attic groaning with possessions, unopened packing cases, lots of trash, some treasure and mountains of dust) you will need to come up with a few long-term goals rather than immediate ones.

A little every day goes a long way

You will feel so much better when you get up in the morning if you have cleared up after your evening meal, taken the dirty dishes into the kitchen, washed and stored them, tidied the living area and sorted out your laundry and clothes for the next day. Equally, on returning from a hard day's work at the office or in the library, the feel-good factor for you and your housemates or partner goes up dramatically if the place looks tidy and clean. It is welcoming and nurturing – it makes you feel better. Even cavemen felt better when the cave looked more like a home than a butcher's shop.

Mess attracts mess – it's a fact. A pair of unwashed pants on the bedroom floor are quickly joined by another couple of pairs – they reproduce easily and before you know it you have a little family. Hold on a minute, though – what if someone pops round unannounced – your mother, a friend or a potential romantic interest perhaps? How impressed will they be when faced with a total mess? Romance can be hard enough to kindle and sustain anyway, let alone with a backdrop of empty beer cans and the unappealing, pungent remains of last night's takeout. The smell of stale food is a highly effective passion killer. Underwear that has hitchhiked its way from the bedroom floor to the living room in a less than pristine condition doesn't even bear thinking about.

How to Use this Book

This book is aimed at a fairly wide audience – male students; young and not-so-young working men, whether single, married or in partnerships; stay-at-home men, both novices and experienced home managers; and all the women out there who want to pass on the art of household management to their menfolk, whatever their age or previous knowledge. Some readers will be new to household management, others may have a little or even a lot of experience. They can derive some satisfaction from already having a few techniques and tips under their belt. Beginners will soon get the hang of things and move speedily from the nursery slopes to intermediate level. By page 80, all of you will be experts in the art and science of household management and ready to tackle a few off-piste tasks.

The key to understanding the principles of household management is to read, digest and implement the advice in *The Little Book of Domestic Wisdom*. Pass on what you learn, what you achieve, even where you do wrong. People like to hear about successes and failures on the domestic front and thereby imitate or deviate.

Since time began, wisdom has been passed down orally from generation to generation. Cavemen and women sat round the fire and taught their young how to keep the hearth warm, how to barbecue the wildlife and make duvet covers from their fur. Wisdom learnt at one's parents' knee led to the Barbecue Age becoming the Iron Age and then the Modern Age (with a few eras in between). Continue the tradition. Do it subtly, though.

Domestic God

 Look out for the Domestic God icon if you want to fast-track to the heart of the matter (or that of your partner).

Don't drag your partner or housemate around the 21st-century cave by their metaphorical loincloths, telling them what to do in a smug, been-there-done-that-ironed-the-dinosaur-T-shirt kind of way. Share your knowledge gently. Share the housework, too (see page 70). Don't fight over it – buy them a copy for their birthday.

Rewarding times

We all need to feel congratulated or pampered from time to time, particularly when we have faced a challenge and successfully tackled it. Make sure you reward yourself (if nobody else is going to do it for you) by patting yourself metaphorically on the back and treating yourself to something that makes you feel good – a new book, CD or DVD, a massage, or a bottle of good wine. Tell someone what you've done. You are feeling better already.

Dirty Devil

Keep an eye out for the Dirty Devil as a warning not to go there, do this, think that, or even suggest the other.

Know Your ...

Bedroom

The bedroom is a private, personal space, in which to relax, sleep, perchance to dream (as the great bard said). It should be a sanctuary, a secure and safe place. Treat it right and you will be rewarded, in one way or another.

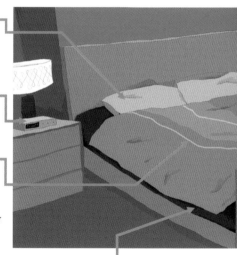

1 PILLOWS
Plump your pillows every day.

2 APPLIANCES
Limit electrical appliances to the essentials.

3 BED BEHAVIOUR
Wash your bedlinen regularly, particularly your pillow case. Make sure your pets know your bed is a no-go area.

4 MATTRESS MANAGEMENT
Turn and vacuum your mattress to keep dust mites at bay.

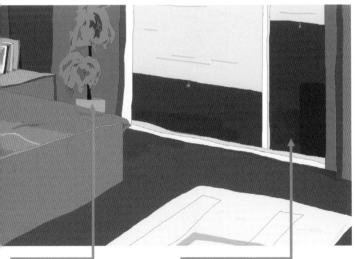

5 PLANTS
They bring a touch of colour and exoticism and help keep the atmosphere healthy.

6 DECLUTTER
Keep bedroom clutter to a minimum. Hang up and store your clothes at the end of the day.

Learn, Earn and Burn

Life is all about learning. Domestic life has its very own learning curves, some steeper than others. To scale and conquer, you need to focus. The art of household management can be divided into three key areas: Learn, Earn and Burn.

Three Small Steps for Mankind

1 LEARN

Learn the principles of housework – not just the 'what' but the 'why', 'how', 'when' and 'where' involved. It is the first big, important step along the highway to hygiene heaven. The *Little Book of Domestic Wisdom* will explain all these aspects. It will reveal the dangers of not cleaning your home, the secret hazards involved and the risks you are running. It will unravel the mystery of an ancient art made simpler by modern technology. Look what happened when Aladdin tried a spot of polishing on the brass lamp. The same new world could open up to you with just a little effort.

2 EARN

Earn the brownie points and reap the benefits, physical, spiritual and emotional, of mastering what are essentially simple but rewarding (in many senses) techniques. Housework is good for you. It helps keep you hygienic and therefore appealing, it brings with it gold stars and brownie points, and it helps put a new, improved shine on that domestic halo you have been hiding under your dusty bushel all this time. Your romantic, emotional health will get a spring clean.

3 BURN

And, lastly, burn those calories as you master this important art. It is cheaper than going to the gym, it doesn't involve a commute and you kill two birds plus a zillion potential allergens and unpleasant germs with one proverbial stone, swoop of the cloth or flourish of the vacuum. Exercise reduces stress, helps trigger the happy hormones and builds muscle. Housework is indoor exercise. You can choose your own time and your own background music. You are never far from a reviving drink or nourishing snack. What more could you want?

THE WHOLE EQUATION

Let's look at the whole equation:

Where
DW+S = **D**omestic **W**isdom plus **S**atisfaction

and
hm = household management
w = weekly
d = daily
cb = calories burned
mb = muscle built

$$DW+S = hm \ (w) + 250cb + mb+1.9\%$$

$$DW+S^2 = hm \ (d) + 500cb + mb+3.5\%$$

 ## Add to this Equation ...

Add to this equation the Domestic God factor and it suddenly starts to add up and make sense. The statistics are even more attractive when you add your potential brownie points (bp) and personal appeal (pa). It is a win-win situation.

Questionnaire

It is time to ask yourself some serious (and some not quite so serious)
questions. Have a go at this quick questionnaire to find out just how much you
do know about the subject of household management. If you get more

Do you know it all already?

**How often should you launder
your bedlinen?**
A) TWICE A MONTH
B) TWICE A WEEK
C) WHEN YOU HAVE A 'SLEEPOVER'
D) WHEN YOUR MOTHER COMES TO STAY
E) WHEN YOUR DOG REFUSES TO SPEND
   THE NIGHT WITH YOU

**Why should you remove dust
regularly from surfaces?**
A) IT GETS UP YOUR PARTNER'S NOSE
B) THERE IS NEVER ENOUGH TO WRITE
   YOUR WHOLE NAME IN
C) IT IS FULL OF DEAD DUST MITES AND
   CAN CAUSE ALLERGIES
D) YOU CAN'T SEE JUST HOW COOL YOU
   LOOK IN THE MIRROR
E) YOU DON'T NEED TO – JUST TURN
   THE LIGHTS DOWN

**How would you describe your
bedroom?**
A) A SANCTUARY
B) A STOREROOM
C) A SHOP WINDOW
D) A NO-GO AREA
E) A SCANDAL

**Is your cat more hygienic
than you?**
A) YES
B) NO
C) IT'S A CLOSE SHAVE
D) ABOUT THE SAME
E) I DON'T HAVE A CAT

**Which items of clothing are on
your bedroom floor?**
A) EVERY PAIR OF SOCKS I OWN
B) MY ENTIRE COLLECTION OF TIES
C) UNSAVOURY UNDERWEAR
D) NONE
E) ONE SHOE, ONE SHIRT AND NEITHER
   ARE MINE

questions right than wrong, you are weaving your way to wisdom but by no means are you an all-knowing, all-powerful household cleaning agent. If you get more wrong than right, you need this book badly.

What equipment is currently residing in your bedroom?
A) A MOBILE PHONE, MINI BAR, LAPTOP, PRINTER, TV, TEASMAID, BREAD MAKER AND DISCO BALL
B) JUST MY ALARM CLOCK AND LAMP
C) A TELESCOPE, CHEMISTRY SET, TRAIN TRACK, SUBBUTEO GAME
D) CAN'T GET IN MY ROOM TO CHECK
E) DRUM SET, SNOOKER TABLE, COCKTAIL BAR, TROUSER PRESS, SAFE, TV, DVD PLAYER, SCANNER AND PRINTER

What activity do you indulge in most in your bedroom?
A) CHILLING, DEBRIEFING AFTER WORK AND RELAXING
B) MAKING PHONE CALLS, WATCHING TELLY AND PLAYING MY GAMEBOY
C) WORKING ON MY LAPTOP IN BED IGNORING MY PARTNER
D) READING, WATCHING AND THINKING THINGS I SHOULDN'T
E) SULKING

How would your housemate describe you?
A) DOMESTIC GOD
B) DIRTY DEVIL
C) DOMESTIC DUNCE
D) DOMESTIC DANGER
E) DON'T HAVE A HOUSEMATE, OR A PARTNER, OR ANY FRIENDS...

Does your choice of shoes reveal?
A) YOUR SHOE SIZE
B) YOUR FASHION SENSE
C) YOUR COLOUR BLINDNESS
D) YOUR LACK OF JUDGEMENT
E) YOUR TOES

What should your shirt match?
A) YOUR EYES
B) YOUR CAR
C) YOUR BANK BALANCE
D) YOUR UNDERWEAR
E) YOUR PARTNER'S

Weekly Wonders, Monthly Miracles, Annual Asks

Establishing a routine for chores is important. It's just the same as at the office – a macro and micro analysis. It helps you see the bigger picture. Consider all the jobs that have to be done and create a list or chart that

Chore Chart:

ANNUALLY:

- DE-JUNK THE WARDROBE, THROWING OUT CLOTHES YOU HAVE NOT WORN IN THE PAST 9–12 MONTHS
- WASH BLINDS
- SHAMPOO CARPETS
- CLEAN CEILINGS AND WALLS
- CLEAN DUVETS (DOONAS), QUILTS AND BLANKETS

MONTHLY:

- TURN AND VACUUM MATTRESS
- CLEAN WINDOWS
- VACUUM THOROUGHLY
- WASH PAINTWORK
- TIDY CLOSET
- REPAIR CLOTHES

divides them into four headings: annually, monthly (or quarterly), weekly (or fortnightly if you are very lazy) and daily. Hourly is taking the whole micro stuff just too far... sticking to a weekly schedule really does work.

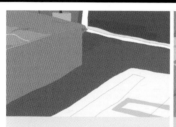

WEEKLY:
- CHANGE BEDLINEN (OR EVERY FORTNIGHT)
- WASH PILLOWCASES
- VACUUM OR SWEEP FLOOR
- DUST SHELVES
- CLEAN SURFACES
- SORT OUT DRYCLEANING

DAILY:
- AIR BOTH BED AND ROOM
- MAKE BED
- SORT AND REMOVE DIRTY LAUNDRY
- HANG UP CLOTHES
- TIDY ROOM
- REMOVE CUPS, GLASSES AND PLATES

Domestic God: Top-to-Toe

Look after your physique before you step out of the bedroom. There is no point making a valiant attempt to keep your home in order if you fail to pay similar attention to your body. Is it not a temple after all? How will you attract people into your pristine lair if you don't look good too?

Top-to-Toe Hygiene Routine

The Eyes Have It

Eyes are the mirror of your mind, the windows to your soul, the first thing a potential mate (house or heart) will gaze into. Treat them with respect. Red eye, black eye, puffy eye – none are attractive. Eat and drink in moderation, get as much sleep as you can (it helps your brain and your body stay in top condition) and trim your eyebrows from time to time or ask your partner to pluck them (but not during the football or when you are trying to end the relationship). The Mad Professor look went out a while back.

Everybody Nose It

Talking of trimming, keep nasal outcrops under control with hair groomers – tweezers are too painful. Examine nostrils before a meeting or date or you could put people off the main deal. Ears need a trim from time to time too. Find a quiet moment in the bedroom. It isn't much of a spectator sport. Moisturize your nose and the rest of your face during the day and at night, particularly during the winter months when your skin is dry and after exposure to the sun. Keep a pot of the stuff next to your bed so you can apply last thing. Men moisturize. It's a commercial fact.

Hair Flair

Hair flair is up there with body beautiful in the premier league of hygiene habits. Keep an eye out while dressing for dandruff and use a clothes brush to remove. Buy a special shampoo dedicated to the task of removing it and hold your head high, shoulders above the rest. Bed-head at the desk, like desk-head in bed, doesn't impress. Have regular haircuts and listen to the opinion of those who have to look at you more than you do yourself. They will advise on the suitability of mullets, ponytails, extensions, hair bands and other accessories. Use the mirror in the bedroom to try out different looks.

Mind and Body Debrief

Keep the bedroom floor clear of clothes and daily debris, and you will be able to relax, meditate and exercise in there. Do some proper breathing to wind down after a hard day at the desk. Deep breath in, deep breath out. Think nice thoughts. Stretch out on the bed or floor and take some horizontal time out. Debrief – literally and mentally. Take your work clothes off – shed the trials of the day as you do so. Separate day and evening in this way.

Body Armour or Amour

If it has been a lean year and you are thin at the waist, tuck in your shirt. If you are expanding in that area and going for growth, wear a jumper (don't tuck that in). Emphasize or lose a size. Don't wear belt and braces at the same time – choose between them. It's like two-timing. Not on, mate. Go easy with flashy buckles and check out tie and shirt combinations in the mirror. If you are colourblind, get advice – daily. Burn your white socks.

Best Foot Forward

Belt and shoes should match. Shoes must be polished and in good condition. A huge number of people make decisions about others based on their footwear. Scruffy and scuffed shoes reflect similar inner traits. They don't say 'try me on for size'. Suede shoes go well with casual wear, but look after them, too. Keep shoes in shape with shoe trees. Air them regularly and change your socks like your underwear (that is everyday, by the way). Don't wear the same pair (shoes or socks) day after day.

Technique Tool Wisdom Cleaning Chore

A Day in the Life of a Bedroom God

OK, we've established that running a household is not unlike running a business. You've probably got the daytime routine more or less under your belt, but you may well be struggling with the best tactics for the evening

Domestic God's Bedroom Routine

6:00pm

ARRIVAL AT MY PLACE INC.
Greet partner, dog, cat, fish with cheery smile. Feed and water where appropriate, prepare chilled wine or hot drink for partner, according to instructions, and then self. Check how partner's day has been.

6:15pm

DEBRIEF
Remove daywear, exchange for casual outfit, hang up work clothes as necessary, after emptying pockets, removing belt and placing money and keys in obvious place. Put shoe trees in shoes and store in wardrobe.

6:30pm

DEAL WITH OFFENDING ODOURS
Collate dirty clothes for laundry. Spray a relaxing scent for emotional debrief. Lie on bed, do physical and breathing exercises. Tidy room. Emerge refreshed and ready to assume multi-tasking evening role.

10:00pm

TYING UP LOOSE ENDS
Iron clothes for next day for self and partner. Polish shoes. Tidy living area, plump cushions, remove old papers and debris, take trash out and wash up cups and glasses. Check pets' and plants' needs.

10:40pm

TIME AND MOTION
Check supplies and prepare shopping list. Take dirty clothes to utility room and programme for overnight wash. Fold clean, dry clothes and place in ironing basket. Place dry-cleaning near front door with briefcase. Lock up.

11:00pm

RETIREMENT PROVISIONS
Prepare for bed, complete bathroom routine, relax in bath, listen to music, give bathroom a quick clean.

agenda. The success of My Place Inc. relies on the same skills, demanding strategy, discipline, motivation and flair. It's now time to apply all of these to a different but just as important routine.

6:45pm

ADMINSTRATION AND REFRESHMENT
Deal with urgent bills, emails,
phone messages. Fifteen minutes of PA per day keeps weekends free. Prepare simple, balanced, nourishing meal for self (and partner).

7:15–8:00pm

PRIVATE CATERING
After demonstrating culinary skills and awareness of importance of healthy regime, wash up dirty dishes and pans, tidy kitchen and wipe surfaces clean. Add up brownie points.

8:00–10:00pm

COMMUNICATION AND THE MEDIA
Relax in living area, engage with partner, sort joint and separate diaries, read papers, watch television, listen to radio or music. Get up to speed in personal, national and international affairs.

12:00–7:00am

REST AND RECUPERATION
Open window slightly, communicate or debrief with partner, sleep as soundly and noiselessly as possible in order to recoup mental and physical energy for 9am-5pm agenda.

7:00am

FAST TRACK OPERATION
Greet partner, air bed, pets. Execute early morning self-cleansing tasks, arrange breakfast for partner, self and pets, make bed, find keys, phone, diary and briefcase and enjoy smooth, stress-free exit.

8:00–9:00am

DELIVERY
Arrive at place of work or study, calm and ready for daytime challenges. Deal with emails, phone messages and urgent memos. Diairize, prioritize, organize. 9am-5pm begins.

Don't be a Bedroom B**

Do you really want to hear the word 'no' in the bedroom? Here are a few
indicators on how not to be a klutz. Read the no-no's and hear a yes-yes.
From no, non, nein to yes, oui, ja in 5!

Domestic God's No-Nos

1. Bed Bugs

Don't try to run your office from bed by
creating a mini HQ between the sheets.
Laptops in bed are a no-no, as are mobile
phones, too many remote controls, brief
cases and work files. Pillow talk isn't
dangerous, so press the Think key and
keep it simple. If you and your partner are
in bed but glued to separate phones, you
are obviously moving along different lines
and action is required.

2. Damp Squibs

Leaving a wet towel on the bed does no
one any favours. It's a careless action
that's both unthinking and unhygienic,
leaving an unnecessary damp patch on
the sheets or bedcover and preventing
either the towel or bedding from drying
and airing properly. It doesn't help the
atmosphere in the room – on any level.
The moisture becomes trapped, unable to
evaporate, thereby creating a perfect
environment for unpleasant microbes and
mould-makers to move in and multiply. It
takes seconds to hang up a wet towel, so
what's the big deal?

Dirty Devil says ...

There are many ways to think dirty
in the bedroom – dirty sheets,
towels, clothes and habits. Dirty
looks will result.

3. Whisk us Away

You can be forgiven for leading pets to
believe they are the most precious things
in your life, but they should be banned
from the bedroom, especially if you suffer
from allergies. Teddies and soft toys
collect dust too, and create clutter, so
don't turn your bedroom into a small zoo.
Animal instincts of a different kind are
fine but no impostors please.

4. Nail it on the Head

Clipping your toenails is unthinkable,
right? It is about the worst personal
habit you could indulge in and impose
on others. Toenails are at the most
southerly point of the body for a very
good reason – that of distance. The
amputated, offending articles should
not be seen anywhere near the bedroom.
If toenails are between the sheets,
romance won't be. End of discussion.

| Technique | Tool | **Wisdom** | Cleaning | Chore |

Bedroom Beauty

You spend a third of your life in bed, but that does not mean you should have a third of your life's possessions in the bedroom. Create a womb-like space not a bomb site. Don't mix the spellings.

✓ Domestic God's Do-Dos

1. Ventilate, not Hibernate

It's important to air your bedroom on a daily basis. Open up those windows, pull back your sheet and blankets (or duvet) and let the room respire not perspire. Try gulping a bit of fresh air yourself. Allow it enough time to circulate and air the bed – get ready for the day, have some breakfast and make the bed and close the window (if you need to). If you have done the unthinkable and smoked in bed, this is even more important. Stuffed animals and stuffed shirts don't go down well in the bedroom and stuffy sheets are a no-no too.

2. Keep it Cool

Humans are like food – best preserved (and served) at the right temperature. In the bedroom we should keep it cool if we want to sleep well. A room should be around 18°C/64.4 °F, a bit warmer for some older sleepers, cooler for others. We don't want to cook at night or freeze, but just enjoy the right degree of comfort to help us sleep properly. There is nothing worse than waking up thinking you are in a walk-in freezer or gently sizzling on the barbie. If you want to be dish of the day, keep the temperature right.

Think safe, secure, serene, sleep – all those 's' words work in the bedroom.

3. Upside Down

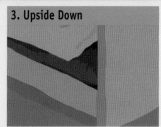

Keep your mattress clean with a mattress protector and wash it regularly (you can buy anti-dust mite covers, too). It is certainly easier to keep sparkling clean than a mattress. Ever tried to hang a mattress on the line? Remember to turn the mattress itself frequently, once a month if possible. It can then regain its original shape and won't end up as a mould of your own body and that of your partner, a living sculpture of your relationship. And you find all sorts of things under mattresses, so it could end up being an interesting exercise.

4. Hang it All

Don't leave your clothes all over the floor, the chair, the bed, the dressing table. It is not a contemporary art installation. Hang your clothes up every evening, using hangers for jackets, trousers and suits, folding your woollens and putting dirty linen in the utility room. Your clothes will last longer (and your relationship might too). Don't try making a smelly sock and underwear mosaic on the floor. Make your bedroom a sanctuary not a slob hole. You may be inviting someone in there soon. Do you want it to be a no-go zone?

Technique

Tool

Wisdom

Cleaning

Chore

Bedroom Confidential

Large it up in the bedroom, guys. Do you want to be a Bedroom Blob or a Sleeping Beauty? There are cool tools out there. Get your hands on some. Don't spend your weekends wandering round the shops. Watch the football

Use or Pose: a Guide to the Stars

Wooden Hanger	Use	Pose
	★★★ Gradually replace your wire hangers with wooden ones, which are wide, shaped and supportive.	★ They protect your clothes from RSI – repetitive stress injury – and ensure that you don't sport extra bumps when you put them on.
Trouser Hanger	**Use**	**Pose**
	★★★★★ Hang your trousers by the cuffs (the bits near where your feet go). Straight-talking, they then take up less room in the closet.	★★★★ You will look more business-like, with crisp, straight lines. Get the edge in the wardrobe and the office.
Padded Hanger	**Use**	**Pose**
	★★ Padded hangers may look precious, but that is exactly what they are. They cost a bit more but save you more too.	★★★★★ They don't look you straight in the eye but they are pretty straight talking.

instead and then pick 'n' choose from the utensils shown here. The team has been selected – all you have to do is get training with them. Some are more stylish than others; some just score.

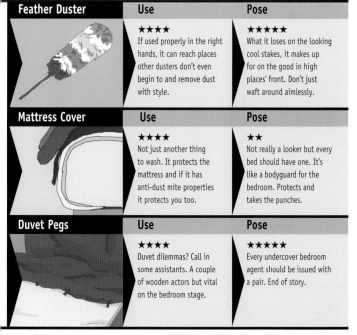

Feather Duster	Use	Pose
	★★★★	★★★★★
	If used properly in the right hands, it can reach places other dusters don't even begin to and remove dust with style.	What it loses on the looking cool stakes, it makes up for on the good in high places' front. Don't just waft around aimlessly.
Mattress Cover	**Use**	**Pose**
	★★★★	★★
	Not just another thing to wash. It protects the mattress and if it has anti-dust mite properties it protects you too.	Not really a looker but every bed should have one. It's like a bodyguard for the bedroom. Protects and takes the punches.
Duvet Pegs	**Use**	**Pose**
	★★★★	★★★★★
	Duvet dilemmas? Call in some assistants. A couple of wooden actors but vital on the bedroom stage.	Every undercover bedroom agent should be issued with a pair. End of story.

Tools: Clothes Care

Hanging, folding, storing – get to grips with all of these new bedroom skills using the tools and tactics shown here. Chucking, abandoning, forgetting are so not cool.

Invest and Prosper

Clothes Brush

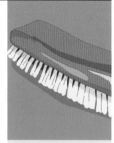

Keep clothes free of hair, surface dirt, soil and (sorry to bring it up) dandruff with a clothes brush. A lint tape roller helps remove the very stubborn fluff. An excellent investment for your clothes portfolio.

Matching Socks

Socks mate for life. That is nature and you have to respect it. Keep them in pairs in the wash, on the line and in your drawer. Don't hurl them in the wardrobe – store them with their partner.

Essential Oil Bottle

Fabric moths just adore wool. The larvae munch the fabric and transform it into a sieve. Clothes you don't wear are the most likely victims as they don't get out much. Try putting a few balls of cotton wool dipped in lavender or rosemary oil in the drawers.

Tissue Paper

It sounds a bit excessive but it really helps to wrap freshly polished shoes in tissue paper before putting them in the case next to your nicely ironed white shirt. Packing clothes with tissue paper between them means you arrive crisp not crestfallen.

Drawer Liners

Use brown paper roll or buy some nicely patterned draw-lining paper. It helps keep your clothes clean. Do what you have to do. Steal your brother-in-law's leftover wallpaper. If you like the idea of scented paper, your clothes will smell even nicer.

Tie Rack

Keep your ties in good condition and save space – all at the same time, using a tie rack that hangs over the wardrobe door. You will be able to select the right tie at a glance instead of rummaging in your drawers feverishly first thing in the morning.

Tools: Just Care

Check out some of these top tools for Best Bedroom Boyz Band. If you want to get the music right in this important room, read on. If you want discord, turn the page and face the music.

Learn and Improve

Mirror

Mirrors reflect well on you in the bedroom and are essential. One quick glance confirms if you are looking acceptable, have breakfast on your chin or tie, are involved in stubble trouble or shaven haven and if that pesky dandruff/nasal furniture is under control.

Bed Cover

Once you have made the bed, put on a quilt, throw or bedcover. It protects the bed clothes from uninvited guests (four- or two-legged visitors in search of a trampoline) and unwanted spillages. It makes the room look tidy.

Sewing Kit

An SSK (sewing survival kit) is an essential piece of bedroom equipment. Needles, pins, safety pins, thread, scissors, a medley of buttons, tape measure and thimble (if you are a wuss). Then get sewing under your belt (so to speak).

Fresh Flowers

Fresh flowers are a bit of a luxury but they improve the atmosphere in several ways. They bring colour, scent and a welcoming feel to what can be one of the less inviting rooms in the house. Vital for the guest room. This way, petal.

Water Jug and Glass

Another essential for the guest room and useful in your bedroom, too. It is a lovely touch for visitors to find a matching set at their bedside. Remember to fill the jug with fresh water (duh).

Fresh Towels

You know all about changing your own towels regularly. If you are entertaining, always supply fresh towels for your guest. Not just dry, dirty ones. That is really horrid. Buy a matching set in your mother's favourite colour.

Tools: Vacuum Cleaner Attachments

When becoming intimate with a vacuum cleaner, you will have to meet its various attachments. It's rather like the early stages of a new relationship. It's important to know who is who and who does what. Alternatively, think of each

Know your Attachments

Crevice Brush

Seek and destroy. Gets into crevices and cracks you didn't know you had. Narrow, tricky, remote and difficult? No, not you – the dirty zone. This will sort things out.

Radiator Nozzle

Good at cleaning radiators, strangely enough. Equally good at zapping dirt and dust on narrow shelves and those areas of the house that normal parts don't reach. Bit of a multi-tasker, in fact.

Upholstery Nozzle

Good at vacuuming sofas, cushions, curtains, mattresses and other furnishings. Yes, you do have to vacuum the mattress unless you want to share your dreams with a zillion dust mites.

attachment as an aspect of your own personality; each one is effective in a particular environment. Don't forget cordless handheld vacuums – great at zapping crumbs with minimum effort, maximum speed.

Dusting Brush

Tackles dust on all sorts of surfaces, whatever shape (due to a 360° swivel action). If it is curved, carved or of cranky camber, this is your man.

Combination Tool

Equipped with versatile, straight suction for smooth or carpeted surfaces and delicate rugs. Like a footballer who can play in defence or attack.

Smooth Floor Brush

Bit of a smooth operator. Focuses on floors such as parquet, stone or vinyl. Gives you a high-five-shine every time. Reflect and smile.

History of the Vacuum Cleaner

Ever wondered who invented the vacuum cleaner? What on earth did people use before it appeared on the market? How did Homo Erectus keep the cave clean and get rid of all those nasty bits of bone on the fur carpet? Well, Mr Erectus probably developed a few good abs and pecs by doing it manually.

From 400,000 years ago until the late 1800s floor coverings were cleaned by being brusquely beaten outside. In 1900, one early Domestic God cum Inventor decided he had had enough of this and tried using a small engine with compressed air to blow away the dust. Sadly all it did was redistribute the dust (as easily happens today when you use a feather duster incorrectly or sweep up without a strategy).

In 1901, a civil engineer known as Mr H C Booth came up with the idea of a machine that sucked up the dirt through a filter and set about making it. His suction machine was big, noisy and had to be manned by four people and parked outside customers' homes, happily before the invention of traffic wardens. After the machine made short shrift of cleaning the carpet in Westminster Abbey, it was snapped up by royal appointment (Edward VII was a big fan) and hand-powered vacuum cleaners swept the market. In 1907, an American by the name of James Spangler invented the first portable vacuum cleaner powered by an electric motor and sold the patent to a company called Hoover. The rest was history until the British inventor James Dyson came up with the bag-less machine in the early 1990s, making a major breakthrough in home cleaning with his dual cyclone system. Next on the agenda is the robot vacuum. You don't even have to stay home and the house will be cleaned without you touching a button or handle. While you save up for one, get a grip on DIY vacuuming.

If you are an all-in-one kind of guy, there are products that profess to be the ultimate in multi-tasking, multi-purpose cleaners with mop heads, built-in wringers, detachable broom heads with powers to generate enough static electricity to lift pet hair from carpets and hard floors. And they can be used to scrub yards, paths and patios. They are the equivalent of the guy who's good at science, art, technology, romance and housework – a 21st-century Leonardo da Vinci with a plug.

Cordless handheld or upright vacuums are extremely useful additions to your household equipment. They are great at zapping crumbs and dirt with minimum effort and maximum speed. Perfect for panic clean-ups.

1 DUST BAG
Most of the dust becomes trapped in the bag while air escapes through pores in the bag.

2 FILTERING SYSTEM
Residual dust is removed from the air by the filtering system.

3 EXPELLED AIR

4 ROTATING FAN
This expels clean air, creating a partial vacuum inside the dust bag.

5 ROTATING BRUSH
Loosens dirt from carpets and rugs.

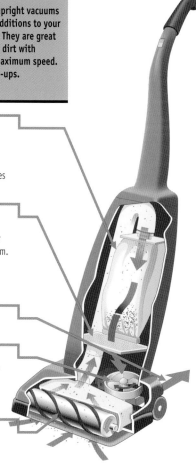

Technique | Tool | Wisdom | Cleaning | Chore

Vacuuming

There are a few important things you need to know about vacuuming. First of all, it is not too time-consuming, particularly if you do it regularly. Vacuuming is not a chore – it is a quick way of making the bedroom and indeed you yourself feel better (really, it is). You can save money by vacuuming – it prolongs the life of your bedroom carpet by preventing dust from settling deep into the fibres and damaging them. In an ideal world you would vacuum every day, but if you just don't have time, focus on the area around your bed.

Low Pec Hi Tech

Before

After

New technology does happen in the cleaning world too. You can now buy special long-handled devices that have removable, replaceable static cloths on the end. They allow you to swish around uncarpeted floors with speed and grace, collecting dust through a static process. It's quick, easy, effective – and more than a little stylish.

Four Facts about Vacuuming

- For some people, vacuuming releases feel-good hormones. For others it has a more negative impact. If you don't mind it and your partner dislikes it intensely, offer to do more than your share.

- Over 70 per cent of people forget to vacuum the edges of carpets and under the bed. You can change this statistic. Dust bunnies thrive in hidden, neglected spots. Zap them before they zap you.

- Just thirty minutes of strenuous dirt-busting will burn around 100 calories. so there's some good bedroom exercise for you!

- Studies of dust allergy sufferers show that minimising exposure to dust mites in the bedroom decreases allergic reactions. If you or your partner is dust-allergic, the best solution is a vacuum with a HEPA (or S-class) filter which blocks small particles of dust and dirt from being circulated in the air.

Suction function

Even bare floors benefit from vacuuming along the grain. Your machine will probably have attachments for specific uses, surfaces and degrees of suction. Read the instructions carefully. As a general rule, think the harder or denser the target fabric, the stronger the suction required.

A clean sweep

For sweeping, a sturdy broom is an effective tool for removing large particles on floors that see lots of action, such as living areas, kitchens, hallways, utility rooms and porches. Use the outside – in principle, again, to avoid aimlessly pushing the dust back into the air. Your aim is to collect the dirt in the centre of the room.

Size does matter and small is useful

A smaller brush can be very handy for sweeping the dirt into the dustpan or getting into tight corners or nooks and crannies. Brush as much dirt as you can into the dustpan and then move it back a little to scoop up the dirt you missed the first time.

The big brush off

Sweeping the carpets is not generally necessary or useful, although you might want to collect stubborn pet hair with a small brush. If you have wooden floors in your bedroom, it's a different matter. You can sweep, dust or vacuum those.

Dusting

Most of you reading this will have little idea of just how smart dust is. You probably ignore it or simply pretend it doesn't exist. Warning, warning – you do so at you peril. House dust is very, very smart. It penetrates every crevice, it lives under the bed, it even creeps into it, and at the slightest hint of a breeze, it becomes airborne – all the better for invading your orifices.

Dust busting

Regular dusting and vacuuming is absolutely essential. Remember you have to control dust mites, too. These are nasty-looking arachnids that are too small for the naked eye. They live on a high protein diet of skin (yours and your pets, mostly) and other organic matter. Their waste matter (faeces and pulverized bodies) can trigger allergies and are not good for those who suffer from asthma. They are not nice housemates and must be discouraged.

Dust is not only found on flat surfaces at eye level – walls also need dusting and cobwebs need removing regularly.

Dusting Techniques

WALL TO WALL OPERATIONS
Dusting is strategic. It's not just a matter of finding an old shirt, ripping it

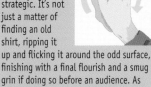

up and flicking it around the odd surface, finishing with a final flourish and a smug grin if doing so before an audience. As with any other exercise, your tools play a very important role. Always use a clean cloth or you will simply transfer the dirt from one surface to the other. If you are dusting walls, use a firm circular motion.

SURFACE TO AIR MISSILES – DON'T GET INVOLVED
When dusting delicate surfaces, don't flex your pecs quite as

much. A firm but gentle action is the way to go – oval or circular is fine for the motion, but it is a wiping not a flicking movement that you are aiming for. Feather dusters tend to lift dust particles and propel them into the air, rather than gathering and removing them (which is the object of the exercise).

Weapons and Tactics

There are a few useful ground rules for dust busting. Pay attention to the don'ts as much as the dos:

TOP TO BOTTOM

Think top to bottom, high to low, up to down. There's no point dusting a low-lying table before you dust the walls – the dust will simply spread.

ADHERENCE NOT DISPERSAL

The mission you have undertaken is adherence not dispersal. You want the dust to stick to the cloth not fly around the room at random.

DUST BEFORE YOU VACUUM

Dust before you vacuum. Unless you enjoy dusting so much you want to do it again.

DRY CLOTH

Use a dry cloth on wooden surfaces and a slightly dampened cloth on others, such as metal or painted surfaces.

COTTON CLOTH

Use a clean, soft cotton cloth or re-use an old (clean) tea towel. Synthetic fibres are not sufficiently absorbent (unless they are special static cloths).

WOOD

Don't get wood damp. Use an impregnated cloth with a dusting aid spray or polish.

CIRCULAR MOTION

Use firm but gentle oval or circular motions. Treat the target with respect. Choose 'lift' rather than 'slide' as a strategy for anything on the surface, such as glass and china ornaments, lamps or knick-knacks of huge sentimental value to you or anyone else.

Mission accomplished. Admire.

De-cluttering your Space

You will know that clutter has reached dangerous levels when you trip over a pile of dirty clothes, slide headlong across a forgotten glossy magazine sprawled on the floor, or spend half an hour looking for your house keys and credit cards first thing in the morning when you have an important meeting to go to. What you need is a concerted attack on the clutter, some useful storage and a reduced level of sloppiness for a more ordered existence.

Cut the clutter

Everything we bring through our front door needs a storage place, either temporary or permanent, or a place in the trash, so here's how to deal with most of the stuff.

Uncontrolled collecting, unnecessary hoarding and sheer laziness when it comes to containing piles of stuff are all enemies of a tidy house. The argument that old reading matter 'might contain some information I need' is often the defence for uncontrolled collecting, while excuses about 'no time to tidy up' often occur in living rooms that don't include enough storage space. Newspapers, magazines and books are space vampires in the bedroom. Old, yellowing papers piled high in a corner or in pieces under the bed are offenders on a number of levels. They are visually unattractive (unless you are an abstract artist working in paper), a potential fire hazard and they steal space. So chaps, gather your loincloths, make the decision to clear the clutter,

embark upon the mission and divide things into the Need and Don't Need piles.

Everthing in the Need pile should be found a home. Think about building in some alcove shelves and a cupboard if essential items such as CDs and magazines remain homeless. Divide the Need pile into stuff you use every day and stuff

you just can't bear to throw away. Much-used items should be found space in an accessible place, others can be stored in the loft, under the stairs or elsewhere.

The Don't Need pile can go in the trash, but preferably recycle items by distributing them to relatives, friends and charity stores.

Crumpled furniture

Beds that look as if an elephant has spent the night on them and then sprawled trampled cushions on the floor during a bad dream, are not appealing. Instead of 'good morning' they say 'bad night.' Abandoned items are not just unsightly, they are also unsanitary and create a 'negative' space.

Keep your bed and any chairs looking smart by plumping up cushions and regular vacuuming. Look under the bed and discover Roman coins, crumbs, discarded food wrappers and pizza boxes.

Tidy up your floor area by hanging up your clothes, putting your shoes away and storing last season's outfits.

Clutter bunnies

Clutter bunnies are experts at creating Might Just Need piles. Don't be tempted by this solution unless you have a proven track record for using such things effectively. If in doubt, ask yourself whether you have ever made a delightful papier mâché bowl out of piles of outdated newspapers or unpaid bills?

Domestic God says ...

The bedroom is a place in which to sleep and dream. It is not a lost and found office.

File not pile. Cut out any really interesting and useful articles as you read your magazines in bed and put them into a reference file immediately – don't simply create another pile. Mind the scissors when you go to sleep. Mini clutter is as unhelpful as maxi clutter, so don't just divide and multiply. Books that you have finished should be returned to the bookshelf or recycled to a charity book store. Sports kit should find its way to the laundry basket or closet. Never stuff it under the bed and forget about it.

Temporary storage

Placing important papers in boxes ready for filing is a form of temporary storage. Collecting together all your photos and storing them in a shoebox in anticipation of arranging them one rainy day in the future, is another useful exercise. Even keeping paperwork and used packaging safely in a designated box for recycling is an effective form of non-permanent storage. If you feel overwhelmed by the idea of de-cluttering all your rooms and putting everything in its final resting place, create some temporary storage and you will feel instantly rewarded.

Cleaning Floors and Windows

Regular vacuuming preserves both your carpet's quality and its appearance, but why not try to minimize dirt in the first place? Use a dirt-trapping doormat at the front door or entrance to the bedroom and rugs or runners in the hallway. Ask people to wipe or remove shoes and boots at the front door.

Move the bedroom furniture periodically (lift not push please) to avoid permanent crushing. Use castors and protectors under furniture legs to prevent squashing the pile. A handy hint that really works for removing dents is to place an ice cube in each one. As the cube melts the fibres swell. Run over the dents with a vacuum cleaner and the wet fibres will become upright again. Neat huh?

Natural is nice

Many people opt for natural floor coverings such as sisal, jute or coir nowadays. They are hard-wearing alternatives and work well in households with small two-legged or four-legged inhabitants. They should be vacuumed regularly

(the floors, not the children or pets) and on both sides if they are rugs (again not the children or pets). Stains are less obvious on such floorings, but that doesn't mean you can leave them. To remove mud or other solids, lift off the excess with care and leave the rest to dry. Brush along the weave with a stiff brush and then vacuum. Liquid spills should be dealt with

swiftly. Blot firmly, working from the outside in. Avoid wetting the area further and don't even think of using a conventional carpet shampoo. For persistent stains, call in the professionals.

Cork floors

If you have a cork floor, take extra care. Vacuum or sweep regularly but resist the temptation to rush off

Solid Hardwood Floors

DIRT, GRIT AND SAND will scratch, dent and dull your floors. Invest in floor mats and keep floors clean. Sweep regularly using a broom equipped with fine ends that can trap the dirt effectively.

PETS with long nails and weak bladders scratch and stain wood. Train your pets and trim their claws (sadly, felt pads don't work on dogs and cats).

LIQUID SPILLS (water, coffee, wine, etc.) left for any length of time on the floor will cause stains. Wipe up spills as soon as they happen.

LADIES with high heels and dangerous stilettos can leave an impression on your wooden bedroom floor. Ask them politely to remove their perilous footwear – everyone will feel more comfortable.

and get the mop and bucket. Remember, cork floors are made from the cork tree and are therefore organic. They need to be cleaned with appropriate specialist liquids and waxes. Ask your local hardware store to advise you. Always deal with spills as soon as they occur. You may well prevent the formation of stains by so doing. Act now, no need to repent later.

Linoleum floors

Linoleum is becoming increasingly popular. Made with linseed oil, ground cork, wood, flour and resins, it is quite

environmentally sound while being comfortable and warm. Amazingly enough, it is also able to destroy bacteria on the floor naturally, leaving you with less work. Cleaning is easy. Just sweep and vacuum thoroughly (but not aggressively) before washing with detergent and warm water.

Rugs

Rugs are a great idea for the bedroom. They can introduce colour to the room while protecting the floor. Anchoring a rug to the floor using a non-slip felt mat equipped with a sneaky adhesive base will

keep it safely in place. Rugs don't escape attack by nasty critters and need to be vacuumed regularly.

Windows on the world

Dusting or vacuuming your window frames and sills regularly is important for their maintenance. Give the paint a wash every month if you can. Think of your windows as the eyes of your home onto the outside world. Light has to filter through the same obstacles in order to enter the room, affecting both its mood and your own. Dirty windows never make a good impression.

Stain Removal

Stains are inevitable within the home, however much care you may take to prevent them, but the quicker you act, the more successful you are likely to be at removing them. Deal, don't disguise. Heal, don't hide.

Stain Removal Kit (SRK)

Every household needs a Stain Removal Kit (SRK) primed for action at any moment. For general household incidents, the following equipment is all you need. Photocopy the list and take it to the store:

- ABSORBENT PAPER TOWELS OR SPONGES
- CLEAN, ABSORBENT WHITE CLOTHS
- ALL-PURPOSE DETERGENT
- WHITE VINEGAR
- WHITE SPIRIT
- BLEACH
- AMMONIA
- NON-OILY NAIL VARNISH REMOVER
- LAUNDRY STAIN PRE-TREATMENT PRODUCT
- SPECIALIST STAIN REMOVERS (FOR THINGS LIKE BALLPOINT OR FELT-TIP STAINS)
- RUBBING ALCOHOL
- BICARBONATE OF SODA
- SOLVENT-TYPE CLEANING FLUIDS OR DRY-CLEANING FLUIDS
- NON-SOLVENT STAIN OR SPOT REMOVER
- LEMONS

FLOORS

Before you set about removing stains from wooden flooring, it is important to ascertain whether the stain or scratch is within the wood itself or just on the topcoat finish.

NATURAL- OR WAX-FINISH FLOORS / FLOORS WITHOUT HARD FINISHES

Gently rub the stain with a damp cloth, rub dry and then wax. Again, the working-from-outside-in principle applies. Water stains should be rubbed with steel wool and then waxed. White rings can be removed using a paste of salt and olive oil left on the stain overnight. Wipe off the next morning and re-wax.

WOOD FLOORS WITH HARD FINISHES OR VARNISHES, INCLUDING POLYURETHANE

Care needs to be taken with such floors (you can detect them by checking to see if the stain is in the superficial finish). Scratches should be repaired with specialist kits available from flooring retailers and other stains should be treated with specialist cleaners for urethane finishes.

Removing a Stain

1

Don't waste time. Grab some paper towel and act. Pulling a rug over the stain won't help. Ignoring it won't make it go away. It's like toothache. Think SBS – scoop, blot, solution. If it's a liquid spill, it's more of a BBS – blot, blot solution technique. Blot with paper towel or a soft, clean and colourfast cloth.

2

If the spill is solid or semi-solid, you need to scoop up as much of it as you can with a spoon, spatula or similar blunt object. Don't use a carving knife – cutting out a stain is not a solution. Be careful to contain the spill. Don't play with it or rub it into the carpet. This is serious stuff and you need to get a grip.

3

Now is the time to apply the cleaning substance. Use a mixture of detergent and water or a specialist stain remover. Read the instructions. It's a good idea to do a test patch first in an inconspicuous spot. Apply the cleaning substance directly to the stain, give it time to do its work and then blot clean.

4

The final tactic is to spray lukewarm water over the offending area and blot as usual. Once the carpet is dry, gently brush or vacuum the area to restore its pile and glory. You may need to repeat this process. If you fancy steam- or dry-cleaning your carpets, call in the professionals.

WALLS AND PAINTWORK

Unwanted scribbling on the walls calls for bicarbonate of soda diluted with a little water in a small bowl to form a thick paste. Rub the paste gently on the offending mark.

Stain removal on wallpaper is a tricky business and you may end up making things worse. Choose from a wide selection of commercial substances, including solvents, but follow instructions carefully and check they are safe for your type of wallpaper. Sometimes, rubbing dirty patches with stale white bread has been known to work (who said household management was predictable).

The Bedroom Routine

Bedding should be aired daily, so you don't have to make your bed as soon as you get up. Instead, pull back the bedcovers (no, don't throw them on the floor) and let everything breathe while you prepare for the day. After breakfast, return to the bedroom, smooth your sheets and blankets, plump the pillows and pull up the cover.

Undress your bed

In an ideal world, you would change your bedsheets and pillowcases every week. If this is not feasible, every two weeks is just about OK, but do try to launder your pillowcases weekly. Remember that it is in the direct firing line of perspiration, tears, oil and saliva for a third of your day.

You may choose to sleep with a top sheet under the duvet (doona), in which case it's quite easy to pop this into the wash along with your pillowcases, or, alternatively, swap the top and bottom-sheets around and make sure you wash the latter every week.

If you use a blanket regularly, make sure that it is dry-cleaned once a year. Take down your feather-filled duvets and pillows to a specialist cleaner annually too. Bedding with synthetic fillings is washable.

Horizontal Harmony

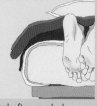

Look after your bed properly and it will look after you. Mattresses have a natural life of around ten years, so if you want a full decade of use, here's what to do: Turn the mattress from time to time, and every three months, turn it top-to-bottom. Vacuum the mattress and pillows regularly. Airing your mattress outside will help keep it fresh and mite-free.

If this is not practical, use mattress and pillow protectors, remembering to launder them regularly. Duvets and pillows should be aired outdoors too occasionally. Take off all the covers, give the duvet and pillows a good shake and leave them in the sun for a couple of hours.

Make Your Bed and Lie in it

A few top tips for making your bed:

Smooth Operator

To prevent a bottom sheet looking and feeling more like a 3D contour map of the Himalayas, ensure your bottom and top-sheets are smooth and wrinkle-free.

Fold it Over

If you like to use a top sheet covered by a blanket, fold the sheet over the blanket at the top so that you don't drool all over it during the night.

Tuck it in

A top-sheet used with a duvet (a doona) or blanket should be tucked neatly and snugly at each corner, over an unfitted bottom sheet. Avoid 'frozen foot syndrome' at 3am.

Duvet Dilemma

Fighting with your duvet or quilt cover as you struggle to fit it is a common source of annoyance and frustration. It is actually quite a simple exercise. Turn the cover inside out and slide your arms inside so that the material is bunched along the length of your arm. Find the corners of the cover, grab the relevant corners of the duvet and slide the cover on, shaking it down as you go. Alternatively, attach pegs to the first two corners as you place the duvet inside and shake down.

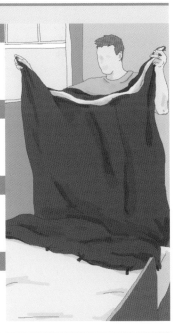

Domestic God says ...

Always fasten your duvet cover before washing in order to avoid socks and underwear running for cover inside it in the rough and tumble of the washing machine.

| Technique | Tool | Wisdom | Cleaning | Chore |

Bediquette

It has been calculated that humans spend around one third of their lives in bed, but this doesn't mean that one third of their belongings have to join them there. The bedrooms should be a womb-like space that provides refuge and sanctuary and the simple essentials needed for our development, just like the real thing.

✖ Bad Bed

A bad bed is unmade, unclean, untidy, unhygienic, uninviting and in some cases unrecognisable as a bed. You won't sleep well in a bed with dirty, crumpled sheets. If it's full of books, videos, magazines and crumbs (and they are just the identifiable objects), you're quite likely to sleep alone, except for the uninvited guests with several legs and even more unpleasant habits. Too much really is *de trop* in the boudoir. Keep the equipment down and your love life might look up. The bedroom should be just for you and your

beloved. Brush the sheets regularly (or simply change them), air the bed and the room every day and put the mess where it

belongs – in the trash or in another room. Compare these images – which room looks the most appealing?

Domestic God says ...

Keep your sanctuary sanitary, your boudoir bug-free, your haven hygienic...

Dirty Devil says ...

For some reason Bedroom Slobs play home matches alone (except for a record crowd of dust mites).

Simplicity is key, so banish random memorabilia, photographs, trophies or childhood clutter and stick to uncomplicated decoration and clean lines. In general, you will feel safer and healthier in a simply equipped and furnished bedroom.

✓ Good Bed

A good bed is clean, tidy, smooth, fragrant, hygienic, inviting and minimalist. Its sole purpose is to offer a sound and healthy night's sleep. Warm it up with a blast of hot air from your hairdryer on a cold night. Make sure your pillows are supportive – they should resume their original shape after you have punched them gently on both sides. Our ability to sleep is greatly affected by our body temperature. Don't sleep under too many bedclothes. Change the weight of your quilt with the season. Just use a sheet when it is hot.

Reduce the contents of the room and bed space to a minimum for maximum comfort. Remember your bed is a safe space in which to relax, debrief, sleep, dream, gather your loins (for later or the next day, depending). Let's keep it clean, guys.

Guest Who's Coming to Stay

It always seems like such a good idea to invite parents, relatives or friends to stay until the day approaches, and you become increasingly anxious. Treat the visit like an important presentation to a potential employer or college lecturer.

How to be Hospitable

- Try to find out when guests are planning a visit. Pre-empt rather then panic blindly.

- If guests arrive on a Friday evening you can relax with them ahead of a whole day together on Saturday and hopefully they will leave after lunch on Sunday.

- Say 'hello and welcome' with a glass of chilled wine or fizz. They will feel special. If they are not, buy fake champagne or beer.

- Arrange an outing – a visit to a local museum or landmark will do. Check out first if history, geology or shopping is their preference.

- Organize a relaxing walk that leads to a charming watering hole. Offer to pay for the first round, expect not to have to.

- If it's a chilly night, light a fire in the living room – assuming there's a fireplace there. If it's high summer, have the barbecue ready. Warmth comes in all forms.

- Remind yourself of their eating habits. A meat fest won't go down well with vegetarians.

The product: My Place Inc. The target market: member(s) of A-list social circle. The strategy: to welcome, win over and generally spoil. The time frame: one day or two evenings. The action plan: implement the following advice, calmly:

How to be the Perfect Host

Don't say Yes to No-No's

Banish no-no's from the living area, dining room, bedroom, kitchen and bathroom. If the utility area and your office are not looking at their best, keep guests out. Whatever part of the cleaning operation you miss, it will be discovered. Prepare for constructive criticism of your proposal.

Don't Panic

Remember, your guest wants to see and spend time with you rather than inspect where you live. If tidiness involves extra temporary storage, then go for it but promise yourself you will sort it out as soon as your guest has gone. If time is short,
focus your cleaning activity on the obvious areas of the most important rooms: their bedroom, the kitchen and bathroom surfaces are top of the list. Washing the curtains and walls are not. For specific operations, check the relevant pages of this book. Enjoy playing host and the 'welcoming' part of the strategy will come naturally.

Welcome to My Place Inc.

Clean and clear the guest room. Remove any inappropriate reading matter from previous occupants, tidy, dust, wipe and vacuum. Ensure sheets are clean and wrinkle-free. Add a few luxuries such as a vase of
flowers, a glossy magazine (check tastes first), fresh fruit or biscuits, sweet-smelling soaps and a fresh fluffy towel on the bed. Turn back the bed covers at night, check the room temperature and always let your guest use the bathroom first. Prepare a tasty but healthy breakfast the next day after delivering a cup of tea and newspaper to the room.

Make Yourself at Home

If guests offer to cook a meal, accept. It will make them feel at home. Their culinary skills might out-do yours.

Spray some lavender scent in their bedroom at night – they will be asleep in no time.

Closet Encounters

Close your eyes, take a mental stroll through your house, opening each door. Which one do you want to close immediately, engulfed by horror and shame? The answer is probably the one that hides the room in which your clothes are struggling to survive, a multi-coloured, mismatched shoal of sardines competing for space and air. Just like humans, clothes deserve respect.

Vertical or Horizontal

Woollen clothes like to be horizontal. Fold knitted garments carefully and keep them on a narrow rather than a deep shelf, or in a drawer with room to breathe. Ensure they are clean before putting them away or the stains will attract moths, keen to convert your clothes into sieves. Hanging up wool pulls it out of shape and can cause hemlines to sag. Ironed shirts on the other hand should be kept vertical – they do not appreciate being stuffed, creased and crumpled in to any old place. Hang shirts on hangers with space between them and they will crease less. Smart move all round.

Before you go to bed, fold and hang your trousers, after emptying all pockets and removing the belt. This avoids sagging and bulging in inappropriate areas and is useful for jacket pockets, too. You could try hanging a complete outfit on one hanger in readiness for the next day, particularly if your partner has a later start than yours and would, for one reason or another, prefer you to dress in the dark. Make sure you keep to your own section of the hanging space, however. It avoids conflict, confusion and comment in the office. Separate full-length and half-length items within your own section. You might even try sub-dividing shirts and suits by colour, occasion or venue – office, evening, formal, informal, restaurant, club, very casual, resistible, irresistible, ski-slope, tennis court, golf course, sauna.

Socks and underwear are happy when horizontal but are easier to identify in the early hours if housed in separate compartments within drawer organizers or dividers. Place a tie rack over an otherwise empty closet door and your complete collection can be seen at a glance while remaining in good condition. Prune it from time to time or it may overflow. Attach hooks and pegs to redundant surfaces and hang belts, umbrellas and bags on them to make space work for you. Shoe racks will help you keep track of your footwear.

Space Odyssey

Get Close and Personal

Closets, like people, benefit from being organized, orderly, logical and hard-working, both vertically and horizontally. Like you, they can become just the opposite. Trousers enjoy tall spaces. What they lose in unfortunate creases, you gain in sartorial stature.

Arms Folded

Fold your woollens and sweaters carefully and store horizontally on narrow shelves. Put those for summer at the top when winter comes, and vice versa.

Store by colour so that you can find the one you want quickly in the morning or when about to go on a date.

Keep Space Alive

Use dead space at the very top of the closet for suitcases and bags. Store boxes at the bottom with stuff inside them to make maximum use of space. Keep spares of things in your suitcase to save time when packing for an urgent business trip.

Open and Shut

Keep socks and underwear in drawers. Again, don't just hurl them in when they are clean and dry. Use dividers to keep them in order – never store socks without their partner. It is just too cruel.

Socks mate for life. That's nature – you have to respect that.

Collared

Always hang your shirts in the closet with enough space between them to avoid creasing. Otherwise, why bother ironing in the first place? Use proper hangers and remove stuff from jacket pockets before suspending. Don't leave clothes in their dry-cleaning bags. Don't cram ties in the drawer. Hang them on hooks or a special tie rack attached to the door. You will find them more easily in a hurry.

Caring for your Clothes

Think of your closet as an investment portfolio. Buy your clothes intelligently and sensibly with a view to long-term rewards and your quality purchases will bring dividends. Buying cheap clothes is a 'fast buck' strategy that can work with your more disposable items of attire. Remember to look after your long-term large investments though – your work clothes and shoes. For the rest, here's what to do:

A serious cull of your clothes always makes you feel good and leaves you with a fresh eye for fashion. Anything lurking within the closet that has not seen daylight for over a year must be a serious contender for the charity or recycling bin. Clothes that are much too small or too large for your physique need to go and you can also wave goodbye to items that need mending but are unlikely ever to see a needle and thread.

If you still lack closet space after a ruthless edit, divide clothes into winter and summer items and find a storage space for next season's range. Put clothes into vacuum-packed bags under the bed, in plastic lidded crates under the stairs or up in the loft. Ensure clothes are clean before you store them. When the next season dawns, apply the above principles of style and ruthlessness before giving them closet space. Always use proper hangers – ones that will not rust and have broad, supportive shoulders – they will extend the life of your clothes.

No-Nos

Never wear belt and braces at the same time. Your choice depends upon where you need support most.

Go easy on the flashy buckle unless you are auditioning for a bit part in a cowboy film. Subtle is the way to go.

White socks and dark shoes were not made for each other. Red is OK for special moments (personal or professional).

Make your own music, guys. A loud shirt is sometimes OK and a statement tie helps the conversation flow.

Fashion *faux pas*

Many women envy the fact that men can simply pull on suit, shirt and tie and rush out of the door in the morning. However, here are some tips to consider:

- Belt and shoes should match – black belt and brown shoes do not.
- Shiny trouser seats are a big no-no. Buy two pairs of trousers per suit to avoid this. Alternating a few suits helps too.
- While a black suit is a reliable choice for most occasions – interviews, presentations, birthdays and weddings – wearing black every day is not a good look. Try wearing a grey or blue suit from time to time.
- Black can make bigger men look thinner and hides stains more successfully.
- If your suit jacket is baggy or obviously wrinkly when you button it up, you need to buy a new one – or else you have picked up someone else's by mistake.
- Scruffy, unpolished shoes reflect similar traits in your character. You may think that 'please take care of me' look is appealing. It really isn't.
- Double-breasted suit jackets should be restricted to slim rather than portly figures and those who are aiming for a classic, more mature look.

Suit Yourself

Recap the strategy for prolonging the life of your suits and protecting your investment:

- PURCHASE TWO (OR, IF YOU CAN AFFORD IT, THREE) SUITS AND ALTERNATE THEM.

- BUY TWO PAIRS OF TROUSERS FOR EACH SUIT TO AVOID SHINY SEAT SYNDROME.

- SEND SUITS TO THE DRY-CLEANERS THREE OR FOUR TIMES A YEAR AND REMOVE THEM FROM PLASTIC PACKAGING THE MINUTE YOU GET THEM HOME.

- USE PROPER HANGERS AND HANG UP BOTH TROUSERS AND JACKET EVERY NIGHT WITH POCKETS EMPTIED, BELT REMOVED, BUTTONS AND ZIPS DONE UP.

- GIVE SUITS SPACE TO BREATHE IN THE CLOSET (AND IN THE SHOWER ROOM TO REMOVE WRINKLES QUICKLY).

- BRUSH AND AIR SUITS REGULARLY.

DIY Sewing Skills

OK guys, now for some rather more delicate hands-on skills. No excuses, don't try the 'I'm all fingers and thumbs when it comes to detailed manual work' line. Fingers and thumbs are just what you need, plus a sewing survival kit. Read on to find out how to avoid finding yourself exposed to the elements, after a button goes absent without leave. A stitch in time saves nine, saves face, saves blushes and saves money. Surgeons use these skills all the time and everyone thinks they are wonderful. You'll soon have it sewn up.

First things first – the Sewing Survival Kit. Keeping a mini kit on hand is an excellent and very practical idea. Put one in your briefcase for conferences and business trips. Pop a version in your rucksack for camping and backpacking holidays and always keep one in the car. A sewing kit is just a small-scale version of a tool kit so here are a few key items to keep in stock:

• PACKET OF NEEDLES OF DIFFERENT LENGTHS AND SIZES

• PINS (RUST-PROOF PREFERABLY, WITH PLAIN OR PLASTIC HEADS)

• PINCUSHION (NOT A FANCY AFFAIR, JUST ONE THAT KEEPS PINS IN PLACE)

• SAFETY PINS (SMALL AND LARGE)

• THREAD (ASSORTED COLOURS, I.E. BLACK, BLUE, WHITE AND BROWN)

• NEEDLE THREADER

• ALL-PURPOSE SCISSORS (SMALL ENOUGH TO FIT YOUR KIT)

• ASSORTED BUTTONS (DIFFERENT SIZES, COLOURS, TWO- AND FOUR-HOLE)

• TAPE MEASURE

• THIMBLE (FOR THOSE WITH A LOW PAIN THRESHOLD)

Remember, a bad workman always blames his tools, so get the best quality kit and you'll be off to a good start. Imagine the embarrassing scenario on the opposite page and you'll be glad to have the sewing skills:

Help! My button's come off and you can see my chest!

Don't panic. Get out your Sewing Survival Kit (SSK) and set about fixing the problem. If you can't find the missing button, find a similar one in your SSK or remove one from a less conspicuous place on the shirt.

Preparation

SHIRT OFF YOUR BACK Only very experienced button-holers will be able to sew a button back on an item of clothing while still wearing it. You could puncture key parts of your anatomy, so do remove the garment before applying your new skills.

MAKE YOUR MARK Using a pencil, mark where the button should go (i.e. its original, now empty, spot).

COLOUR COORDINATION Choose a thread colour that matches or is slightly darker than the shirt fabric.

AN EYE FOR DETAIL Thread your needle with a generous length (61 cm/24 inches) of medium thread, using the needle threader.

1	2	3	4

1 TIE A KNOT IN IT
Tie a knot at the end of thread to keep it in place when you make your first stitch. When experienced, you can make one or two small stitches instead.

2 BUTTON IT
Place the button in position (centred over the chosen spot). Insert the needle into one of the holes from the wrong side of the button and bring the needle up.

3 LOOPING
Insert into the hole next to it, passing through from the right to the wrong side of the fabric. Repeat this process a few times, but don't make it too tight or you won't be able to do up the shirt.

4 RIGHT AND WRONG
Take the needle through to the wrong side of the fabric and secure by making a small stitch, inserting the needle through the loop and pulling it tight. Repeat and cut.

| Technique | Tool | Wisdom | Cleaning | Chore |

Suitcase Savvy

If you're hopeless at packing and always seem to arrive at the airport like a bad-tempered beast of burden while everyone else has smart, compact luggage and a smug smile, no worries. Buy a lightweight suitcase and follow these tips:

Think of a Number and Halve It

Put out all the clothes you plan to take with you on your bed and divide them into piles of underwear, socks, shirts, T-shirts, trousers and jeans, shoes and sneakers, sweaters etc. Now halve each one, except for the underwear pile. This is the amount you really need.

Dark-coloured clothes are practical, as minor stains will be less obvious, but they're less suitable for hot destinations.

Let's Not Get Heavy

Pack your heaviest items (shoes, books and toiletry kits) along the spine of the suitcase. Put folded socks, underwear and rolled up belts in your shoes. Place shoes in protective bags to avoid soiling neighbouring clothes with debris or polish. Take miniatures of your toiletries. Decant shampoos and other potions into small plastic bottles then wrap them in plastic bags to avoid leakage. Wear your bulkiest jacket and footwear to save space.

Suit Yourself

Some people like to use suit bags when they travel. There's no folding involved and you can take your proper hangers with you. To pack a suit, first fold the jacket sleeves over the back and then fold the jacket in half. Turning the jacket inside out before folding is an option. Line the bottom of your suitcase with a pair of trousers, creases in place, leaving the legs to dangle over the edge. Pack the rest of your clothes on top, lighter garments last, and then fold the trouser legs over the pile or fold trousers neatly in three, aligning inner and outer leg seams first so that you get a proper crease at the front.

Get Shirty

Shirts should be neatly folded and packed at the top of the case to avoid crushing. Always place flat items over bulky clothes. Pack some good hangers too as hotel ones are often very flimsy. Place breakables in bubble wrap.

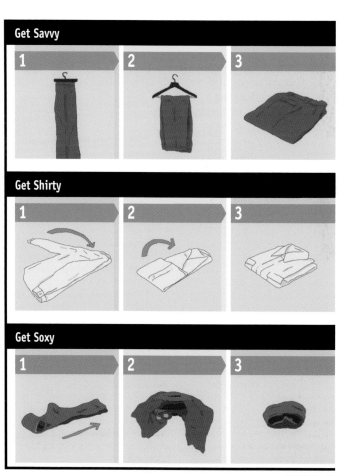

Get Savvy

1

2

3

Get Shirty

1

2

3

Get Soxy

1

2

3

Flower Arranging for Men

Brighten any bedroom with blossoms. Men do flower arranging – it's a fact. Actually, it's a historic fact going way back to the 16th century. Women came to the art later than men. Ikebana, the Japanese art of arranging flowers aesthetically, was originally the preserve of royalty, Samurai families and monks from major temples. The arrangement represents the sky, the earth and man in balance and it is a complex art with specific rules and a deep philosophy. Sometimes it can be a single flower (that sounds good doesn't it?). The lines rather than the colour are emphasized.

Flower Arranging

Arranging flowers is not as tricky or time-consuming as you may think. It can be quite satisfying and may bring out the artist in you. For a basic arrangement, buy a bunch of colourful flowers at a store or florist and pop them gently into a vase (with water). Before purchase, check that the flowers look as if they will have some life left in them on the day they are due to impress your guests. Don't go for firmly closed buds on the morning of your guest's arrival. A warm room will help them open but you need to give them a proper chance over a day or two to open out fully.

Braver folk can try their hand at a spot of floral DIY. Think of the following arrangement as a menu for a simple meal using just three ingredients – in this case anemones, tulips and twisted hazel stems. You can be equally successful using different stems and other flowers, depending on what's in season.

1

- TALL GLASS VASE
- 3 OR 4 STEMS OF TWISTED HAZEL (OR WILLOW)
- ANEMONES (BLUE, ONE BUNCH)
- TULIPS (YELLOW, ONE BUNCH)
- WATER

A Few Tips about Flower Arranging

- Take a couple of vases home – a tall, thin, cylindrical one for long-stemmed blossoms, and a shorter, rounder one for more vertically-challenged groups.
- Invest in some marbles or pebbles (or steal your nephew's collection) and put them at the bottom of the vase to hold stems in place. Colourful glass can look very attractive.

- Strip the stems so that no leaves are in the water. Put water in (duh!).
- Cut the stems to about twice the height of the vase.
- Cross the stems to create a grid that keeps the stems firmly in place.
- Put the longest stem at the centre.
- Arrange the others evenly around it, thinking lines and colour as you go.

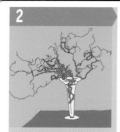

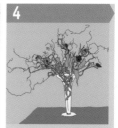

2
Place twisted stems in the vase firmly. Think of them as the backing group. Here come the pop divas. By the way, if twisted stems are hard to come by or you forget to buy, pop out into the nearest forest and collect some attractive twigs. Very *au naturel*.

3
Place the anemones one by one among the twigs, followed by the tulips. Distribute the colour evenly. Don't bunch the blues to one side and the yellows to the other. This is an integrated arrangement not a contest.

4
The tulips may well change shape and position the next day and you will need to adjust accordingly. Place arrangement on bedside table and mention casually if nobody spots it. Flowers bring colour, scent and perspective to the room.

Technique

Tool

Wisdom

Cleaning

Chore

Petiquette in the Bedroom

Pets are wonderful things. Medical studies have shown that they keep us healthy and calm. Cats and dogs (and fish too – who knows?) are always delighted to see you. However, with a pet come additional responsibilities. Suddenly, it is not all about you and your partner or housemate any more. The pitter-patter of tiny feet covered in mud and carrying things into the bedroom from the road, field or backyard can be heard in the air. Don't let your pets sleep on the bed or, worse still, under the duvet unless you want to share your dreamworld with fleas and ticks and other beasties.

If you have to leave your pet while you go to work make sure that you know which rooms Felix or Rover will be in. A few house rules need to be established. If you leave your home full of tempting items, dangerous plugs and cords and the TV remote control just a hop, skip and a jaw-bite away you will not be as happy to see your pet when you return as he or she is to see you. Remember, a large, excitable dog in a tiny apartment is not a love match.

Helpful Hygiene

- Limit your pet's visits to your bedroom. No fake animals or too many real ones in there please. Both are hygiene hazards.

- Wash your bedding thoroughly if your cat or dog manages to climb on your bed. If your hamster or guinea pig manages it, call *The Guinness Book of World Records*.

- If your dog does sneak into the bedroom and leave you an unpleasant message, punish him immediately. He won't know why you are cross if you don't do it straight away.

- If he grabs your socks and won't let go, leave the house and ring the bell. He will drop everything. Don't follow suit.

- If you suffer from allergic conjunctivitis, try wearing sunglasses during special moments with your pet. They won't laugh at you.

Do-Dos

Invest in your Pet

A wise investment generally leads to dividends. Consider it a 'petfolio.' Spend time with your pet each day, buy it toys and chews, install a padded perch near a sunny window for your cat or a comfortable place for your dog to relax. Plant cat grass in indoor pots for your feline friend so it can graze. Buy a ready-made cat tree for climbing opportunities. A happy pet is more likely to be a safe one.

Breed Needs

Do some serious research about the breed of dog that suits your circumstances. How much space, time and energy can you devote to it? Think about the pet rather than yourself when you do this.

On all Fours

Scan your home for possible hazards – shoes, smelly socks, important documents, expensive briefcases, chewable computer wires and cords, designer footwear. Pick up and store or protect all of the aforementioned items.

No-Nos

Dust, Wipe and Vacuum

This tried and trusted trio plays an even more important role in households with pets. If you don't have time to indulge in these three activities twice a week, perform them as often as you can to control hair and allergens. Vacuuming will rid your home of pet fleas, which are fairly common. Place particular focus on the area in and around where your pet sleeps.

Fire, Flames and Fur

Never leave your pet alone in a room with a lit candle or an unattended fire. Animals are attracted to the bright lights and can knock the candles over, spilling hot wax and creating a fire hazard.

Mind Muddy Paws

Don't let muddy paws create a new pattern on your carpet. Wipe paws before they have a chance to make a mess, or invent some shoes for dogs.

Here's Lurking at You

Our ancestors way back slept in animal furs in caves. History doesn't have to keep repeating itself, however, and things are a definitely more hygienic nowadays. However, it is important to keep house dust mites and bed bugs at bay. Make your relationship with them a short one. Meet and greet – 'Howdy, bloodsuckers and faeces feeders,' and then zap, dump and say your goodbyes – 'Make my day, Staphylococcus. You're history, mate.' Keep the air clean in your bedroom. No smoking, swearing or caveman-like behaviour.

Clean and tidy

Next time you are in bed and about to switch the lights out, scan the room and consider its contents and layout. Perform a mental check of how you feel – restful, anxious, claustrophobic, a bit overwhelmed by all the stuff you alone or you and your partner have accumulated? Is there just too much of it? Try removing some of the clutter, a little every day, first thing in the morning and last thing at night. It's surprising how your mood will improve. Limit electrical goods to the minimum, keeping only things that are strictly necessary or have a positive effect on you.

Banish redundant or little-used equipment such as a television set, music system, computer, radio, foot spa and exercise bike. Discard the things that attract more dust than attention and keep only what makes you feel good. Everything should justify its share of the space. Remember, less clutter, less dust, less effort, more time to relax. Great result.

Keep it light and airy

Damp, poorly ventilated spaces make perfect environments for nasty little mites, allergens and bedbugs to flourish, so introduce clean air into the bedroom at regular intervals. Open the windows as often as you can. Allow the room to gulp in fresh and positive supplies of oxygen and expel dust. Airing your bedding is a good idea, too, and sunlight helps to do this while zapping dust mites and lifting your mood, thereby killing two birds and a million critters with one helpful stone.

Keep the room temperature relatively cool and don't smoke in bed – fumes and nasty smells both linger and offend. Don't hang up your wet clothes to dry in your room. Remember your bedroom is a sanctuary for you and your relationship and should be respected as such. Don't pollute it unnecessarily either with noise such as snoring (if you can help it), loud music, phone calls and smelly clothes. The KISS (Keep It Simple, Stupid) rule, if ignored, can result in exactly the opposite.

The oxygen of love
Relationships need space and room to breathe just like real rooms. Csluttered or unhealthy, oxygen-starved atmospheres won't help them flourish. During your sleeping hours, your body takes in oxygen and emits carbon dioxide (exactly the reverse of plants, in fact); you sweat, exude oils, shed skin. It's all perfectly natural so don't be embarrassed, but do take action to avoid the atmosphere becoming stale, dusty and singularly uninviting.

And this is my room...
Introducing someone to your inner space for the first time, whether with platonic or romantic intent, is an act of intimacy, not unlike allowing someone to take a peek inside your underwear drawer. Imagine what they may find, what their first impression would be and whether they would ever fancy another look.

Don't Bug Me!

Did you sleep well last night? You might want to clean up your nocturnal act a bit before getting back into bed tonight. You may have shared your very personal space with up to 2 million dust mites. Bed bugs lurk there too, keen to suck your blood and cause itches and rashes. Bacteria with long, difficult names such as staphylococcus and enterococcus are ready to do their unsavoury thing at any time, causing throat infections and diarrhoea respectively if not respectfully. You wouldn't want to introduce them to your partner with names like that would you? Vacuum your mattress regularly if you want to sleep alone.

Every year, humans shed about 500 g (1 lb) of skin scales. Next time you buy a packet of flour of this weight, imagine it full of skin. Double it if you have a partner. Mentally chuck in a few cans of perspiration and bodily oils and you will quickly see the need for bedroom hygiene.

| Technique | Tool | Wisdom | Cleaning | Chore |

Shortcuts

Prepare to Score (on the Domestic Field)

Maximum score in minimum time. How does that sound? Tempting? 10 out of 10 in 10 minutes takes some beating, guys. Here's a set of Top Trump Tips. Go from hero to zero in no time at all.

10 out of 10 in 10

1 A DUST IN TIME

You will spend a third of your life asleep. Assuming this is mostly in your own bed, you will spend more time in this space than any other. Make sure you keep it clean and it will return the favour – offering a haven in which to sleep and dream away a third of your life. It takes less than ten minutes to give it a good dusting and vacuuming.

2 AMO, AMAS, A MATTRESS

Vacuum the mattress itself every couple of months. Strip the bed entirely, removing sheets and mattress cover (you do have one, don't you?). Use the crevice nozzle to give the mattress a good going-over. Vacuum your bare pillow, too. Dust mites are in the mattress, sheets, curtains, furniture, floors and bedding. Zap them wherever they lurk.

3 IRON OUT THE PROBLEM

When buying bed linen, make sure you check out what it is made of. Pure cotton sheets tend to wrinkle more than those made of a cotton and polyester mix. It only takes a minute to read the label. Ironing is not compulsory, of course, and if you dry the sheets on the line, pegging them nicely tight and taught, you can avoid getting the iron out.

4 ABOVE AND BELOW THE LINE

If you use the space under your bed for storage, make sure you can remove stuff easily and give the area a good vacuum. Use boxes or trays that slide them out without difficulty. Don't use this area as an alternative waste paper bin. Make sure you get rid of old coffee cups, glasses, chocolate wrappers, pizza boxes and other debris from under, on and beside the bed.

5 IT TAKES NO TIME AT ALL

Stop smoking. It is as simple as that. Give up cigarettes. How else to put it? Most importantly, stop smoking in the bedroom. It is unhealthy, unhygienic, unfair (on your lungs and your partner's), it pollutes the air, it is a fire risk – just stop it. OK? Nothing more to be said. Except to add that you should give up smoking in the entire house, guys.

6 SUN, SUN AND SUN

The sun is a bit like another pair of hands in the house. Take your blankets outside and give them a good dose of sunlight to keep dust mites at bay. The blankets will smell nicer too. This is not a substitute for cleaning but a reinforcement strategy. If you could get your mattress out into the garden on a sunny day that would be great too.

7 COOL, CALM AND QUIET UNTIL...

You are asleep, your partner is asleep. And then it starts. The sleep-shattering, relationship-threatening snore. You don't know about it because it is coming from your part of the bed. If you are a big snorer, try to investigate the cause. It could be to do with alcohol, weight, sleep position or a physical problem. Take time to look at www.britishsnoring.co.uk

8 PLAYING AWAY OR OUTDOORS

If you visit friends and stay the night, take a duvet cover with you and sleep inside it. Save your hosts the effort of washing the bed linen before and after your stay. It's useful for putting inside your sleeping bag when you are camping to save you extra washing. If you have a heavy night and can't find a pillow, inflate the wine box foil bladder and use that.

9 SLEEP DIARY

If you have difficulty sleeping, it could be due to anxiety, stress, emotional overload or your partner's snoring (read Tip 7). Keep a sleep diary to diagnose your own body clock and sleep patterns. Make a note every day for a month – when you feel sleepy in the evenings, when you go to sleep and wake up. You will see that this is the time you should retire.

10 GO TO BED WITH LAVENDER

A relaxation session before going to sleep is a perfect way to send you off. Ask your partner (nicely) to treat you to an essential oil massage – try a lavender-based diluted massage oil. Ask your partner to focus on particular areas of tension (shoulders, nape and back are usual culprits) and then the rest of your body. Lavender is good for stress, too.

| Technique | Tool | Wisdom | Cleaning | Chore |

Do It Together

It is true that a problem shared is a problem halved. It applies within relationships and within the home. Give your relationship 100 per cent. Put in your 50 per cent. It's a simple equation. What other deal would give you that sort of return?

It is reasonable for one partner to expect the other to do their share of the household tasks. Share the chores and share the joys. Partnerships work better when respect and care are involved. Always being the one to strip the bed and vacuum the floor is not going to make you feel respected and cared for. It's another quite simple equation. It may make you feel resentful and upset, taken for granted. That's not good for relationships, romantic or platonic.

We have established that housework keeps you healthy, brings rewards, spices up your love life and makes you more attractive. Divide and drool. Don't just talk about it – it's Chore, Chore not Jaw, Jaw.

Why not draw up a list of the household tasks that need doing and work out who does what, who hates what, who doesn't mind what. Too big an ask? Too much like

 Domestic God says ...

If you know your partner really dislikes one particular job, put L or DM. That's compromise. Uh-oh another 'C' word.

hard work? OK, guys, here it is, all done and dusted (well, actually you have to do that bit).

Photocopy the page and then fill in the boxes as follows – one of you uses the photocopied page (don't argue now!):

L = Like
H = Hate
DM = Don't Mind

Have a look at the completed charts and share the chores so that you have equal amounts of dislikes and likes (no cheating now guys). Do deals on the Don't Minds.

Add any jobs that are missing and apply to your particular circumstances. This exercise is part of the whole process of domestic democracy. Don't start the Chore Wars – be a Domestic Diplomat and do your bit for world peace.

 Dirty Devil says ...

If you know your partner really likes one particular job, you may be tempted to put RL against it. That's naughty!

Domestic Democracy

Chore	Like	Hate	Don't Mind
DUSTING			
VACUUMING			
POLISHING			
TIDYING UP			
WIPING SURFACES			
AIRING THE BED			
CHANGING THE SHEETS			
CHANGING THE PILLOWCASES			
MAKING THE BED			
TURNING THE MATTRESS			
PUTTING STUFF IN THE CUPBOARDS			
HANGING UP CLOTHES			
SORTING DIRTY CLOTHES			
DEALING WITH DRY CLEANING			
REPAIRING CLOTHES			
TIDYING DRAWERS			
ORGANIZING MAGAZINES			
SORTING BOOKS AND CDS			
VACUUMING UNDER THE BED			
EMPTYING THE TRASH BIN			
WASHING THE WALLS			
WASHING WINDOWS			
CLEANING THE SKIRTING BOARDS			
SWEEPING THE FLOOR			
CLEANING THE WINDOWS			
CLEANING BLINDS			
WASHING CURTAINS			
REPLACING BULBS			
CHANGING PLUGS			
CARING FOR PLANTS			
RECYCLING			

Wise Dude Mess Mantra

You will know that clutter has reached dangerous levels when you can't find a clean shirt in the morning, when all your ties have mated in a snakepit on the floor, when your sports kit is in a pre-match huddle in the corner, or when you slide headlong across a forgotten glossy magazine. What you need is a concerted attack on the clutter, some useful storage and a reduced level of sloppiness for a more ordered existence.

Organizing the Chaos

Once you have sorted your belongings into piles and graded them into levels of need, you can start to dump, rehouse or store. While temporary storage is good for short term items, you should assess your living space and decide where permanently required objects need to go.

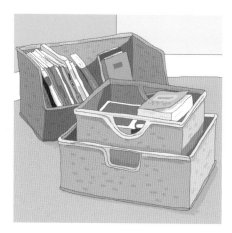

Look on storage as a flexible friend. A mixture of freestanding pieces and built-in units is often the answer for housing all those books, photographs, cosmetics, clothes and shoes. Consult a few magazines or makeover programmes for ideas about which cupboards, drawers, stacking boxes and tables can best answer your needs. Ask a friend whose taste you really admire to come into your boudoir for a consultation. Offer to cook a meal in return for a spot of stylish and effective clutter and storage advice. 'Come up and see my piles some time,' you'll say. Who could resist? If said friend does resist, look through the style magazines and identify a look that appeals and would suit your bedroom.

Mess Mantra for the Bedroom

BUG
EVICTION
DAWNS.   **H**YGIENE'S
REGRET   **Y**OUR
OR   **G**ATEWAY   **E**NJOY
OUST   **I**NTO   **Q**UITE
MESS   **E**XTREMELY **U**NIQUELY   **H**EALTHY
          NATURAL   **A**TTRACTIVE **A**ND
          EXPERIENCES **L**ATERAL   **V**ERY
                       SOLUTIONS **E**XCITING
                                 NEWS

De-ciding and de-termining to de-clutter and de-junking in the bedroom are vital for so many reasons. Look at it from the point of view of a prospective visitor (your mother, perhaps) or potential room mate or putative romantic interest. Gaze around your lair as if you were seeing it for the first time through the eyes of a newcomer or guest.

Employ all your senses. Remove items that offend both visually and nasally. Keep your radio/alarm but move your all-round sound system, CD player, television or plasma screen, MP3 and DVD player, laptop and anything else that could emit a sound and offend the ear into the living area. Touchy-feely items such as football memorabilia, teddy bears, hairy rugs, anything made of fur – fake or real (what were you thinking?) must move to new accommodation too.

All those old magazines, books under the bed, sports paraphernalia etc. must be contained (use a nice basket or box) or else hitch a ride out of town. Create a room Shakespeare would look at and be inspired to say 'Sleep, perchance to dream...' and hope that something happens before the sleep bit...

Technique Tool **Wisdom** Cleaning Chore

QED → QAD

QED (*Quod erat demonstrandum*) – people say and read this Latin expression every day (OK, every now and then). 'That which was to be demonstrated' – posh for proof is in the pudding and we've got the pudding, now (for those not in the know yet). Well, in this case, it is QAD (*Question, Answer, Danger*) or watch out 'cos the pudding might be poisoned. The Danger could be a Beware Bugs, an

Q	A	D
I have just bought a new mattress so presumably I can relax on the turning the mattress front for a while?	No. Look after it from day 1, not after it is too late. A mattress needs care and commitment too.	No. Dust mites are better than Ferraris. They can go from 0 to 200 mph (mites per hour) without you even having to put your foot down.
I like to sleep with the windows firmly closed. My partner says it's dangerous to be so hermetically sealed. Who is right?	If it's too hot, neither of you will sleep properly. Why not compromise and air the room in the morning/afternoon.	Humidity, condensation, dust mite statistics – reduce all these risks. Beware Bugs.
I like to sleep with lots of blankets on and my partner likes the lightweight bedding. Who is right?	Choose the best for both your needs – your partner could just sleep under the duvet and you could add a blanket. Try compromising.	Make sure the heavy- versus lightweight argument doesn't turn the bedroom into a boxing arena. That is the only danger.
My partner and I have to buy a new mattress. Can't we just get one on-line and have it delivered?	No, you must try it out first, and as for as long as possible.	You will have too many uncomfortable nights if you choose the wrong mattress. Remember you will sleep together every night for years.

74 LITTLE BOOK OF DOMESTIC WISDOM

Allergen Alert, an early No Go To Sleep Zone warning. The questions will alert you to dangers lurking in the bedroom that you may never even have thought of, bacteria to which you have yet to be introduced, hazards of which you have until now remained blissfully but not hygienically unaware. Sorry to enlarge your circle of foes. Meet, greet and delete. That's the idea.

Q	A	D
My beloved wants our Norfolk Terrier, Twiggy, to sleep on the bed while I am away for a month on business. Is this OK?	No, it is not OK and nor is going away for so long.	Do you want dog hair, faeces, paw dirt and possibly fleas to greet you on your eventual return? Beware Bugs and Allergen Alert.
I have shelves full of trophies, medals and memorabilia from my football hero days. Are they dangerous?	Yes. Why not put them all in a special cabinet in the living room (or loo).	All of these accessories are potential dust-bunnies and demand extra damp-dusting. Beware Bugs and Allergen Alert.
I'm not getting enough sleep but I'm so busy and don't get to bed till midnight and I'm up again at 6am. Is this a problem?	Yes. Try to get as much sleep as you can. Go to bed and get up at the same time each day, exercise in the morning and avoid caffeine at night.	Too little sleep on a regular basis is not good. It affects the immune system. You may end up irritable, tired and unable to concentrate.
My new partner says I have too much furniture in my bedroom. What's the problem?	More furniture equals more housework. Is that the problem, perhaps?	Each piece will introduce dust into the bedroom. Reduce dust and dusting.

| Technique | Tool | Wisdom | Cleaning | Chore |

A Miscellany of Domestic Wisdom

This page is for dipping into whenever you feel the need for words of wisdom, for whatever reason, whether to motivate yourself or your partner, impress your in-laws or outlaws, chat up a new acquaintance, liven up conversation at a dull dinner or simply amuse yourself in bed. Unlike food at a midnight feast in the dorm, double-dipping is safe. Think of it as a fondue of wisdom, free for all to dip in and out of and back again (not too cheesy?).

Domestic wisdom from the man and woman in the street

A crisp, well-pressed shirt, clean, matching socks and shoes in which you can see your own reflection are the marks of a man in charge of his own destiny.
Sir Roger Barrons

A Lieutentant in the Laundry can be a Captain in the Kitchen and a Brigadier in the Bedroom. He will still await promotion in the Bathroom.
A Ellis

My idea of household management is to sweep the room with a swift, exhausting, all-embracing glance.
Charles Fipps

A piece of paper can be good or bad news. A pile of paper is always old news.
Emily Moseley

Don't invest so much time and emotion at the office that you have none left for the bedroom.
Peter Hanigan

You will encounter emotional vampires at the office during the day. Fight space and oxygen vampires in the bedroom when you get home.
Jane Hanigan

Bedroom Safe, Bedroom Wise

The battle against dust is made harder by having carpets and several pieces of furniture in the bedroom. A hardwood or linoleum floor makes dust control easier. Shagpile is the dream house, the deluxe residence of every dust mite with a wish list. Take this into account before selecting your floor wear. Keep bedroom furniture to a minimum – a chair and bedside table should do it. Dump the headboard or keep it scrupulously clean.

Boudoir curtains require much more attention than you might feel inclined to give them. Vacuum them (how does every couple of months sound?) or, better still, wash them a couple of times a year. First things first, buy lightweight, washable curtains rather than heavy, velvet affairs. Avoid Venetian blinds (so much more dusting involved) and go for the easy care solution.

What you see is not what you get with dust mites. They are invisible. For something so small, they wreak huge havoc, particularly with those prone to allergic attacks or asthma. Just to give you an idea, half a teaspoon of house dust contains around one thousand dust mites and unspeakable quantities of faeces. There are more dust mites in the bedroom than in any other room in the house and they munch merrily on our dead skin, swilled down with a dash of Perspiration Nouveau. It is the protein in the shed skin casts that triggers the asthma problems. Keep it clean, guys. See how on page 66.

Wisdometer

Check battery-operated smoke alarm weekly and electric ones every month. Replace batteries twice a year. Put it on the chore chart. Keep the grille of the smoke detector clean, too.

Always check the manufacturer's instructions on equipment. The booklets are included for a purpose. *Nota Bene*, mate, or buy a Latin Dictionary. Check how to use a fire extinguisher and where plus how to install, test, use and maintain.

Always check safety instructions for electrical equipment and keep all the literature in one safe place – leaflets, guarantees and emergency phone numbers.

Check regularly for bare wires on appliances. If you spot one, turn off, unplug and sort the problem. Always check that plugs and leads are not near heat, flame or water.

Index

Do you know it all already?

QUIZ ANSWERS

HOW OFTEN SHOULD YOU LAUNDER YOUR BEDLINEN?
B

WHY SHOULD YOU REMOVE DUST REGULARLY FROM SURFACES?
C

HOW WOULD YOU DESCRIBE YOUR BEDROOM?
A

IS YOUR CAT MORE HYGIENIC THAN YOU?
B

WHICH ITEMS OF CLOTHING ARE CURRENTLY RESIDING ON THE FLOOR OF YOUR BEDROOM?
D

WHAT EQUIPMENT IS CURRENTLY RESIDING IN YOUR BEDROOM?
B

WHAT ACTIVITY DO YOU INDULGE IN MOST IN YOUR BEDROOM?
A

HOW WOULD YOUR HOUSEMATE DESCRIBE YOU?
A

DOES YOUR CHOICE OF SHOES REVEAL?
B

WHAT SHOULD YOUR SHIRT MATCH?
A